YOUTUBE
FOR PROFIT

THE COMPLETE GUIDE TO MONETIZING YOUR CHANNEL

BENJAMIN WILLIAMS

Copyright © 2022 Benjamin Williams

All rights reserved

The characters and events portrayed in this book are fictitious. Any similarity to real persons, living or dead, is coincidental and not intended by the author.

No part of this book may be reproduced, or stored in a retrieval system, or transmitted in any form or by any means, electronic, mechanical, photocopying, recording, or otherwise, without express written permission of the publisher.

Cover design by: Benjamin Williams

CONTENTS

Copyright	
Introduction	2
Chapter 1: A New Breed of Millionaires	5
Chapter 2: Money, Money, Money!	18
Chapter 3: Cost Per Mille (What?)	26
Chapter 4: Ads!Ads Everywhere!	37
Chapter 5: Alternative Ways of Making Money	46
Chapter 6: But Wait, There's More!	54
Chapter 7: Sell! Sell! Sell!	62
Chapter 8: YouTube Extras	71
Chapter 9: Don't Forget	77
Conclusion	79
Thank You Readers	80

BENJAMIN WILLIAMS

YouTube for Profit:
The Complete Guide to Monetizing Your Channel

INTRODUCTION

Welcome to the exciting world of YouTube monetization! As a creator, you have the opportunity to turn your passion for creating content into a profitable career on the world's largest video sharing platform.

With over 2 billion logged-in users visiting YouTube every month, the possibilities for reaching and engaging with a vast and diverse audience are endless. Many studies have been released stating that young children are looking to move away from traditional careers in an attempt to become YouTubers and Vloggers.

Though a lot of people initially create a YouTube channel out of passion, today we are looking to *monetize* it. That's not to say you cannot have both, I honestly believe for long-term success you *need* both, but monetizing a YouTube channel can be a great way to turn a hobby into a profitable business, and with the right approach and strategies, it is possible to earn a significant income from the platform.

In this book, we will delve into the various ways you can make money on YouTube in 2023. From advertising revenue and sponsorships to merchandise sales and Patreon, we will explore the many monetization methods available to creators and provide helpful tips and best practices for maximizing your earnings in an increasingly *saturated* market.

I use the word saturated not to frighten, but to allow you to follow the correct path to success. Essentially, the key to success on YouTube is to consistently provide value to your audience and to approach monetization with a long-term mindset. By focusing on building a strong and engaged audience, creating high-quality and relevant content, and leveraging the right monetization strategies, you can turn your YouTube channel into a profitable and sustainable business.

Sustainable is another word I want you to remember throughout your time as a creator. Both trends and rules change constantly on the platform, so you must keep in mind that it takes time and effort to build a successful and profitable YouTube business that can weather any changes. Don't be discouraged if you don't see immediate results - building a loyal and engaged audience takes time, it can take months, even years sometimes, but eventually, you will make it.

I always advise those I am speaking with that in addition to creating solid foundations, you will need to be open to trying new things and experimenting with different monetization strategies. What works for one creator may not work for another, so it's important to find what works best for your unique channel and audience.

By focusing on building a strong and engaged audience, creating high-quality and relevant content, and leveraging the various monetization options available to creators, you can turn your YouTube channel into a successful and profitable venture.

CHAPTER 1: A NEW BREED OF MILLIONAIRES

YouTube has become a platform where people from all walks of life can make a living, and even become millionaires (with some top tier creators making their way towards the billionaire status). Understandably, there are quite a few reasons why and how YouTube has been able to create so many millionaire creators.

The first reason is the sheer size of YouTube's user base. As I just mentioned earlier, there are now over *2 billion* monthly users, or 25% of the entire world's population using and accessing YouTube. Sit back and really comprehend that number. YouTube has a massive audience that creators can tap into. This large audience combined with the ease of creating and uploading videos makes it possible for creators to reach a wide audience and build a substantial following.

We also need to remember that there is the variety of monetization methods available on YouTube. Creators can make money through *advertising revenue, sponsorships, merchandise sales, Patreon, YouTube Premium*, and *affiliate marketing*. This gives creators multiple ways to monetize their content and earn a living from their videos.

In addition to the size of the audience and the variety of monetization methods, YouTube's algorithms and recommendation system also play a role in the success of creators. YouTube's algorithms can help creators reach a wider audience by recommending their videos to users who are likely to enjoy their content. This can help creators grow their channel and increase their earnings.

Like most things, I have found that hard work and dedication are the key to success on YouTube. Many of the creators who have become millionaires on the platform have done so by consistently creating high-quality and engaging content, promoting their videos, and engaging with their audience. By putting in the time and effort, you can build a successful channel on YouTube and achieve financial success.

Should I Focus More on Making

Content or Monetization?

This is a question I am asked quite often, and when it comes to making money on YouTube, the question of whether to focus on creating good content or on monetization is an *important* one. Ultimately, the answer depends on your goals and priorities as a creator. There are a few things to consider when deciding whether to focus on creating good content or on monetization:

If your primary goal is to create high-quality and engaging content that resonates with your audience, then focusing on creating good content should be your priority. By creating content that is interesting, informative, and entertaining, you can build a loyal and engaged audience who will be more likely to watch your videos and share them with others. This can help you grow your channel and increase your reach, which can lead to more opportunities for monetization.

On the other hand, if your primary goal is to make money from your YouTube channel, then focusing on monetization might be more important. There are several monetization methods available on YouTube, such as advertising revenue, sponsorships, merchandise sales, Patreon, YouTube Premium, and affiliate marketing. By focusing on monetization, you can identify the most effective monetization strategies for your channel and optimize your content and promotion efforts to maximize your earnings.

Often when I am reading other guides or non-fiction books on simply making money on YouTube, to me they come off as soulless and more often than not they rely on "scammy" behavior to get as much money as possible, as quickly as possible, utilizing tactics that may/will get your account banned eventually, locking you out from creating an Adsense account again in the future.

I do hate to generalize, and this isn't always the case obviously, but from my own experience, I find doing something you are at least semi-passionate about radiates through your work and will create sustainable and lasting success. I know the topic of my book clearly states YouTube for Profit, and I do believe through these methods you can find sustained and worthwhile profit.

Just to reiterate, it is possible to focus on both creating good content and monetization at the same time. By creating high-quality content that resonates with your audience and implementing effective monetization strategies, you can achieve both goals and build a successful and profitable YouTube channel.

Remember, whether you should focus on creating good content or on monetization depends on your goals and priorities as a creator. Both are important for building a successful and profitable YouTube channel, and it is possible to focus on both at the same time.

Things to Consider When Monetizing Your Channel

There are several factors to consider when trying to make money on YouTube. Some will be more important to others, while some may not need to consider these at all. There are numerous cases of YouTubers almost falling backwards into sustainable monetization. However, for us mere mortals, the following may prove useful in some way or another.

YouTube's eligibility requirements

In order to monetize your videos and earn money on YouTube, you must meet certain eligibility requirements, such as having a minimum number of subscribers and meeting YouTube's guidelines for content.

Your audience and content

To maximize your earnings on YouTube, it's important to have an engaged and loyal audience who are interested in your content. Creating high-quality and engaging content can help attract and retain viewers, which can increase your earnings potential.

Your monetization strategy

There are several monetization methods available on YouTube, such as advertising revenue, sponsorships, merchandise sales, Patreon, YouTube Premium, and affiliate marketing. It's important to choose a monetization strategy that aligns with your content and audience and to regularly review and optimize your strategy to ensure that you are maximizing your earnings.

Your brand and image

As a creator on YouTube, your brand and image are important for attracting and retaining viewers and building a loyal following. It's important to establish a clear and consistent brand identity and to maintain a professional and respectful image to help build trust with your audience.

Legal and compliance issues

It's important to familiarize yourself with YouTube's guidelines and any applicable laws related to monetization, such as those related to disclosure and sponsored content. It's also a good idea to seek legal advice if you have any questions or concerns.

Branding and YouTube

In my own experience, the best and most lasting way to monetize effectively is to prioritize providing value and maintaining a *consistent* brand experience. This book will give you a basic understanding on how you can monetize this brand. My other books (hopefully) have taught you how to focus on building a strong and lasting brand, and how to use online tools to grow your business.

Specifically in this book, I will try and convert you to the idea that instead of merely aiming for high video views or a large number of followers, you should focus on cultivating a small, dedicated group of loyal and engaged fans who will actively promote your brand. As a Youtuber, this means putting your energy into fostering relationships with the 10% of your audience who are your most ardent supporters.

By positioning yourself as a "micro-celebrity" on platforms like Youtube, you have the potential to earn enough to achieve financial freedom.

One example I like to use is as follows:

Let's say if you start a *Let's Play* channel and are able to build a small but loyal fan base, you may be able to generate more income from selling products or courses to your fans than you would from ad revenue alone, which can often be hit or miss. Some months you will receive more, others a lot (lot) less, and it is hard to rely on it as a consistent income unless you are a very large YouTuber.

Back to our example.

Even if Youtube pays you a low rate of $0.01 per view (it almost never will), you would still need **200,000** views to make *$2,000*. That is a solid video by most people's metrics, a pipedream for most.

Now, on the other hand, let's say you have built a relatively small but loyal audience, they enjoy your content and your gaming style. You can go a couple of routes (as we will discuss later). But for this example, we can make an 'unboxing video' with a sponsored branded partnership deal as a jumping off point.

The script could look like something as simple as:

Intro:

Hi, everyone! It's [YouTuber's name] here, and today I'm super excited to share with you my new gaming PC from [sponsored brand]. I've been dying to get my hands on one of these babies, and I'm finally able to do it thanks to the amazing team at [sponsored brand].

Segment 1: Unboxing and setup

So, let's start by unboxing the PC. As you can see, it comes in a sleek and stylish packaging, with all the components securely protected inside.

Inside the box, we have the PC itself, a keyboard and mouse, a manual, and all the necessary cables.

Setting up the PC is super easy. All I have to do is plug in the power cord, connect the keyboard and mouse, and turn it on.

And there we go! The PC boots up smoothly, and we're greeted with a clean and intuitive interface.

Segment 2: Hardware and specs

Now, let's take a look at the hardware and specs of this PC. As you can see, it's packed with top-of-the-line components that are sure to provide an amazing gaming experience.

The processor is an [X] from [company], which is known for its excellent performance and power efficiency.

The graphics card is a [Y] from [company], which is capable of handling even the most demanding games with ease.

The PC also comes with [amount] of RAM and a [size] hard drive, so you won't have to worry about running out of space or memory anytime soon.

Segment 3: Gaming performance

Now, let's see how this PC performs in some games. I've picked a few of my favorites to showcase the capabilities of this PC.

First up, we have [game 1]. As you can see, the game is running smoothly with no lag or stuttering. The graphics are crisp and the colors are vibrant.

Next, we have [game 2]. Again, the performance is top-notch, with no issues whatsoever. The frame rate is stable and the controls are responsive.

Finally, we have [game 3], which is known for being one of the most demanding games out there. But as you can see, this PC is more than capable of handling it, with no dips in performance whatsoever.

Conclusion:

So, there you have it! This new gaming PC from [sponsored brand] is an absolute beast when it comes to performance, and it's definitely worth considering if you're in the market for a new gaming PC. Make sure to check out [sponsored brand's] website to learn more about this PC and other great products they have to offer. Thanks for watching, and I'll see you in the next video!

Now, on each stream, within most of your videos you are going to mention your custom-built PC and the brand. From this video and the constant reminders to your audience over a period of a year you sell 100 gaming PCs in a year and make a profit of $250 per unit, you could potentially earn **$25,000**.

As you can see it is therefore often more lucrative to focus on building a dedicated and engaged audience rather than simply striving for high view counts.

Your Loyal Audience

Building an audience is crucial for making money on YouTube because it is the foundation of your monetization efforts. Without an audience, it can be extremely difficult to generate any income from your videos. Throughout this book we will explore the various ways in which building an audience is important for making money on YouTube. As I mentioned earlier, we discuss creating a brand to build that audience, in this book we will assume that you have your audience, or planning on having them soon and wanting to monetize them.

I will say, don't feel bad about looking at monetizing them. You may feel guilty at first, but you are putting in the effort, you are making the content and (hopefully) you are providing them a service worth paying for.

First we will consider the role of advertising revenue. Advertisers pay creators for the opportunity to reach their audience through ads on their videos. The larger your audience, the more valuable your channel becomes to advertisers, which can lead to higher ad revenue. This means that building an audience is important for increasing your income through advertising.

Next, we will discuss different methods such sponsorship deals and merchandise sales. These monetization methods are often based on the size and engagement of the creator's audience. The more subscribers and views you have, the more likely you are to secure sponsorship deals and sell merchandise. This means that building an audience is important for increasing your income through sponsorships and merchandise sales.

Patreon and YouTube Premium are subscription-based monetization methods that rely on building a loyal and engaged audience who are willing to pay a monthly fee for exclusive content and perks. This means that building an audience is important for increasing your income through Patreon and YouTube Premium.

Remember, building an audience allows you to build a community of loyal and engaged followers who are interested in your content and are more likely to engage with your videos and social media posts. This engagement can lead to more views, subscribers, and revenue. This means that building an audience is important for increasing your income through engagement.

How much can I expect to make from YouTube?

It is difficult to predict how much you can make from YouTube, as it can vary significantly depending on a number of factors, including the quality and popularity of your content, the number of views and engagement you receive, and the effectiveness of your monetization strategies.

Some YouTube creators are able to make a full-time income from their channel, while others may only earn a small amount of money.

In general, the amount of money you can make from YouTube depends on a combination of the following factors.

The number of views your videos receive

The more views you receive, the more money you can potentially make (duh).

The number of clicks on ads

When ads are shown on your videos, you will earn a portion of the revenue based on the number of clicks they receive.

The cost per thousand impressions (CPM) of your ads

This is the amount that advertisers are willing to pay for every 1,000 views of an ad. Higher CPM rates can lead to higher earnings.

Your monetization strategies

There are several ways to monetize your YouTube channel, including through ads, sponsorships, and merchandise sales. The more effective your monetization strategies, the more money you can potentially make.

Your audience demographics

Advertisers are willing to pay more for ads that are shown to certain demographics, such as people in certain age ranges or geographic locations. If your audience fits into a desirable demographic, you may be able to earn more from your ads.

It is important to keep in mind that earning money on YouTube takes time and dedication. It is not uncommon for new creators to take several months or even years to build up a large enough audience to start earning significant income from their channel.

CHAPTER 2: MONEY, MONEY, *MONEY!*

More often than not, the best way to earn money is to simply use what is already on offer; the absolute goal of most YouTubers, *Adsense*.

AdSense is a program that allows YouTube creators to earn money from ads shown on their videos. It is one of the main monetization options available to creators on the platform, along with sponsorships, merchandise, and fan funding. AdSense can be a good way to earn supplementary income as a YouTube creator, but it is not likely to be a primary source of income on its own.

The amount of money you can earn through AdSense depends

on several factors, including the number of views your videos receive and the amount of time viewers spend watching them. Advertisers pay higher rates for ads that are shown to a larger and more engaged audience, so if you have a popular and well-respected channel, you may be able to earn more through AdSense. However, it is important to keep in mind that the ad rates available through AdSense can vary significantly, and it is not uncommon for creators to earn very little from their ads.

I would also argue that in addition to the size and engagement of your audience, the quality and relevance of your content also play a role in determining your AdSense earnings. Advertisers are more likely to pay higher rates for ads shown on high-quality, relevant content that is likely to appeal to their target audience. Therefore, if you focus on creating high-quality, engaging content that is relevant to your audience, you may be able to increase your AdSense earnings.

Choosing The Best Monetization Strategy for My Channel

Something I initially struggled with was deciding on the correct monetization strategy for each of my channels. There are several factors to consider when choosing the best monetization method for your YouTube channel. Here are some tips to help you make the best decision.

Assess your audience

Consider who your audience is and what they might be interested in. For example, if you have a gaming channel with a younger audience, you may be able to monetize through merchandise or fan funding.

Evaluate your content

Consider whether your content is suitable for advertising and whether you are comfortable with ads being shown alongside your videos. If you have a channel with sensitive or controversial content, ads may not be a suitable monetization option.

Look at your channel's performance

Consider your channel's view counts and engagement levels. If you have a large and active audience, you may be able to monetize through sponsorships or partnerships.

Explore different monetization options

YouTube offers a range of monetization options, including ads, sponsorships, merchandise, and fan funding. Explore these options and see which ones might work best for your channel.

Keep an eye on trends

As with any business, it's important to stay up to date with industry trends and changes. Keep an eye on what other creators are doing to monetize their channels and consider whether these strategies might work for you.

Advertising Revenue

Earning money through advertising revenue on YouTube is the most popular way for creators to monetize their content and turn their *passion* into a *career*. This is the goal for most YouTubers who do not think outside the box when it comes to monetization (this is slowly changing though). I often like to think of advertising revenue as a constant trickle or stream. Sometimes there will be a deluge and it will outperform other monetize methods, whereas more often than not it will be the butter on the bread so to speak.

I have comprised below a simple step-by-step guide on how to make money through advertising revenue on YouTube. I like to be clear with my instructions so this will allow for the basic foundations.

Step One

Enable monetization for your channel

In order to start earning money through advertising revenue, you must first enable monetization for your channel. To do this, you must be at least 18 years old or have a parent or guardian set up an account for you if you are under 18. You must also have a Google AdSense account linked to your YouTube account. Finally, your channel must have at least 4,000 public watch hours in the past 12 months and 1,000 subscribers. Once you meet these requirements, you can enable monetization by going to the "Monetization" tab in the "Channel" section of YouTube Studio.

Step Two

Optimize your channel and videos for ad monetization.

To maximize your earnings from advertising, it's important to optimize your channel and videos for ad monetization. This includes using appropriate tags and descriptions, creating engaging and high-quality content, and promoting your videos to a wider audience.

Step Three

Monitor your earnings

Once you have enabled monetization and optimized your channel and videos, you can monitor your earnings through the "Monetization" tab in YouTube Studio. Here, you can see how much money you have earned from advertising and get detailed reports on the performance of your videos.

Step Four

Alternative monetization methods

And finally, in addition to advertising revenue, there are several other ways that you can make money on YouTube, such as through sponsorships, merchandise sales, Patreon, YouTube Premium, channel memberships, and affiliate marketing. By leveraging these monetization methods and creating compelling content, you can potentially earn even more money on YouTube.

AdSense Rules

When a creator enables monetization for their channel, ads will be displayed on their videos and the creator will earn a portion of the revenue from these ads. In order to be eligible for monetization, a creator must meet certain criteria such as being at least 18 years old, having a Google AdSense account linked to their YouTube account, and having a minimum number of public watch hours and subscribers.

The amount of money a creator can earn through advertising revenue depends on various factors including the type and length of the ads, the number of views their videos receive, and the number of clicks on the ads. To maximize earnings from advertising, creators can optimize their channel and videos for ad monetization by using appropriate tags and descriptions, creating engaging and high-quality content, and promoting their videos to a wider audience.

Something that is the first big hurdle for creators is making advertising revenue through YouTube. Simply look at any forum or blog and this will be a very common question and point of conversation.

In order to make money through advertising revenue on YouTube, you must first enable monetization for your channel. This has a very specific set of requirements outlined by YouTube. You must meet the following requirements:

1. You must be at least 18 years old or have a parent or guardian set up an account for you if you are under 18.

2. You must have a Google AdSense account linked to your YouTube account.

3. Your channel must have at least 4,000 public watch hours in the past 12 months and 1,000 subscribers.

Seems easy enough right? It can be for some, others it can literally take years. For a large portion of my readers, this will be their primary goal - reducing the time between creating their channel and getting approved for monetization.

Once you have met these requirements, you can enable monetization for your channel by going to the "Monetization" tab in the "Channel" section of YouTube Studio.

When you enable monetization, ads will be displayed on your videos and you will earn a portion of the revenue from these ads. The amount of money you earn will depend on several factors, including the type and length of the ads, the number of views your videos receive, and the number of clicks on the ads.

Remember, once everything has been set up, in order to maximize your earnings from advertising, you can optimize your channel and your videos for ad monetization. This includes using appropriate tags and descriptions, creating engaging and high-quality content, and promoting your videos to a wider audience.

CHAPTER 3: COST PER MILLE (*WHAT?*)

Cost per Mille (translated to 1,000 in latin, French and Italian) or CPM, is a term used to describe the cost that advertisers are willing to pay for every 1,000 views of an ad. Essentially it is the cost per thousand impressions. It is a key metric in the world of digital advertising, and it plays a significant role in determining how much money YouTube creators can earn from their videos.

So, how does CPM work on YouTube? When a viewer watches a video on the platform, an ad may be displayed before, during, or after the video. If the viewer clicks on the ad, the creator of the video will earn a portion of the revenue generated by the ad. The amount of money that the creator earns is determined by the CPM of the ad.

For example, let's say that an advertiser is willing to pay a CPM of $10 for their ad. This means that they are willing to pay $10 for every 1,000 views of their ad. If a YouTube creator's video receives 100,000 views and the ad is displayed to all of those viewers, the creator would earn $1,000 from the ad (100,000 / 1,000 x $10 CPM = $1,000).

There are several factors that can impact the CPM of an ad on YouTube. One of the most important factors is the quality and relevance of the ad itself. Advertisers are more likely to pay higher CPM rates for ads that are well-targeted and engage the viewer effectively. The demographics of the viewer can also impact CPM, with advertisers often willing to pay more for ads that are shown to certain age ranges or geographic locations.

As we have discussed, in addition to CPM, YouTube creators can also earn money through sponsorships and merchandise sales. These additional sources of revenue can help to supplement the income earned through ads and increase the overall earnings of a YouTube channel.

Ultimately, CPM is an important factor to consider for YouTube creators looking to monetize their videos. By understanding how CPM works and how it can impact their earnings, creators can make informed decisions about their monetization strategies and potentially increase the amount of money they make from their channel.

Does CPM Vary Between Niches?

The CPM of an ad can vary significantly between niches and videos due to a number of factors, including the quality and relevance of the ad, the demographics of the viewer, and the competitiveness of the advertising market.

One of the main factors that can impact the CPM of an ad is the quality and relevance of the ad itself. Advertisers are more likely to pay higher CPM rates for ads that are well-targeted and engage the viewer effectively. For example, an ad for a luxury car may have a higher CPM than an ad for a basic household item because the former is likely to appeal to a more targeted and affluent audience.

The demographics of the viewer can also impact CPM, with advertisers often willing to pay more for ads that are shown to certain age ranges or geographic locations. For example, an ad for a product that is targeted towards young adults may have a higher CPM when shown to a viewer in that age range compared to an older viewer.

In addition to the quality and relevance of the ad and the demographics of the viewer, the competitiveness of the advertising market can also impact CPM. In a highly competitive market, advertisers may be willing to pay higher CPM rates in order to reach their target audience. On the other hand, in a less competitive market, advertisers may be willing to pay lower CPM rates.

Below we have a list of 30 YouTube niches that have the potential for high CPM, or cost per thousand impressions. The CPM of a video is determined by the bid from advertisers; the higher the bid, the higher the CPM. These niches represent some of the most expensive options for advertisers based on their low and high bid amounts.

Current CPM Approximates:

1. Email marketing (~$35)
2. Insurance (~$32)
3. Real estate (~$30)
4. Website hosting (~$29)
5. Ecommerce software (~$26)
6. Charitable donations (~$25)
7. Legal services (~$20)
8. Credit cards (~$16)
9. Online gambling (~$15)
10. Ecommerce (~$13)
11. Mortgages (~$11)
12. Search engine optimization (~$9)
13. Online businesses (~$8)
14. Virtual private networks (~$8)
15. Loans (~$7)
16. Cryptocurrency (~$6)
17. Drop shipping (~$5)
18. Home repair and improvement (~$4)
19. Weight loss (~$4)
20. Content creation (~$4)

Finding My Niche

So, your niche wasn't on the higher CPM list, time to quit, I guess. Remember, there are so many factors that both affect CPM and how much money you can make from your channel.

If, however you are looking to focus on a niche that isn't the same as your current passion, there are tools that can assist in helping you find a new direction.

Google Keyword Planner is a tool that can help you find niches with high CPM on YouTube by providing data on the search volume and cost per click (CPC) of specific keywords. Here is a step-by-step guide on how to use Google Keyword Planner to find more niches with high CPM:

Step One:

Go to the Google Ads website and sign in to your account. If you don't have an account, you can create one for free.

Step Two:

Click on the "Tools" tab and select "Keyword Planner" from the dropdown menu.

Step Three:

On the Keyword Planner page, click on the "Search for new keywords using a phrase, website, or category" option.

Step Four:

In the "Your product or service" field, enter a keyword related to the niche you are interested in. For example, if you are interested in the health and wellness niche, you might enter "fitness" or "nutrition."

Step Five:

In the "Your landing page" field, enter the URL of a relevant landing page or website. This can help Google Keyword Planner provide more accurate data on the search volume and CPC of the keywords you are interested in.

Step Six:

Click the "Get started" button.

Step Seven:

Google Keyword Planner will generate a list of keywords and related data, including the search volume and CPC for each keyword. You can use this data to identify niches with high CPM potential by looking for keywords with a high search volume and high CPC.

Keep in mind that while CPC is not directly related to CPM, it can be a good indicator of the overall value of a niche to advertisers. Niches with high CPC tend to have higher CPM potential, as advertisers are willing to pay more for ads in these niches.

It is also important to note that the CPM value of a niche can vary significantly depending on a number of factors, such as the quality and popularity of the content, the effectiveness of the monetization strategies, and the demographics of the audience.

As such, it is important to consider a range of factors when identifying niches with high CPM potential.

Geographical Location

Something I never necessarily paid too much attention to was how geographic location can affect the CPM of an ad on YouTube. I may have made more if I made content which targeted these countries specifically, however I do feel that may have cut into both my quality and authenticity. If you are however able to do so without losing this quality, we can discuss looking at geographical CPM below.

One way that geographic location can impact CPM is by influencing the demographics of the viewer. Advertisers are often willing to pay more for ads that are shown to certain age ranges or geographic locations. For example, an ad for a product that is targeted towards young adults in the United States may have a higher CPM when shown to a viewer in that age range and location compared to a viewer in a different age range or location.

Furthermore, in addition to influencing the demographics of the viewer, geographic location can also impact the competitiveness of the advertising market. In some locations, the demand for ad space may be higher, leading to higher CPM rates. In other locations, the demand for ad space may be lower, resulting in lower CPM rates.

Which Countries have Highest CPM?

It is difficult to accurately identify specific countries with high CPM, or cost per thousand impressions, on YouTube. CPM is the amount that advertisers are willing to pay for every 1,000 views of an ad, and it can vary significantly depending on a number of factors, including the quality and popularity of the content, the effectiveness of the monetization strategies, the demographics of the audience, and the cost and competitiveness of the advertising market.

Moreover, the CPM of an ad can vary within a single country due to differences in the demand for ad space and the demographics of the viewer. It is therefore not accurate to generalize the CPM of an entire country.

According to the International Monetary Fund 2022, the top 10 richest countries in the world are the United States, China, Japan, Germany, United Kingdom, France, India, Italy, Brazil, and Canada, with GDPs ranging from $18.6 trillion for the United States to $1.5 trillion for Canada. These countries represent a wide range of geographical locations and cultures, and they all have strong economies that contribute significantly to the global market. If you are able to target your ads to these countries, you may be able to earn more through CPM due to the higher purchasing power of their citizens.

It's important to note that targeting ads based on geographical location is just one factor to consider when trying to optimize your CPM earnings, and you should also consider factors such as the type of content you are creating and the interests of your audience.

Calculating Your Own Channel's CPM

To calculate your YouTube CPM, or cost per thousand impressions, you will need to know the total number of ad impressions your videos have received and the total amount of money you have earned from ads. You can then use the following formula to calculate your CPM:

CPM = (Total ad revenue / Total ad impressions) x 1,000

For example, if you have earned $100 in total ad revenue and your videos have received 50,000 ad impressions, your CPM would be calculated as follows:

CPM = ($100 / 50,000) x 1,000 = $2 CPM

Keep in mind that your CPM may vary significantly depending on a number of factors, including the quality and popularity of your content, the effectiveness of your monetization strategies, the demographics of your audience, and the cost and competitiveness of the advertising market.

Can I Increase My YouTube CPM?

There are several strategies that YouTube creators can use to potentially increase their CPM, or cost per thousand impressions. CPM is the amount that advertisers are willing to pay for every 1,000 views of an ad, and it is a key factor in determining the revenue that YouTube creators can earn from their videos.

The best way to increase your CPM is by *increasing engagement* with your audience. Advertisers are more likely to pay higher CPM rates for ads that are well-targeted and engage the viewer effectively. By creating high-quality and engaging content, you can increase the value of your channel to advertisers and potentially improve your CPM.

Another great way to increase CPM is by *targeting specific niches*. Some niches may have higher CPM potential due to the demand for ad space and the demographics of the viewer. By targeting these niches, you may be able to increase your CPM.

Something that I spoke about in my first book was *Collaborating with other creators*. Collaborating with other creators can actually help you reach a wider audience and potentially increase your CPM. You can consider collaborating with creators who have a similar target audience or who produce content in a complementary niche. For more on this check out my first book where I give practical examples on how to do this.

Finally, I would also try my best to utilize *YouTube Analytics* to increase CPM. Use the data provided by YouTube Analytics to understand your audience and identify opportunities to improve your CPM. For example, you can use the data to identify the demographics of your audience and target your content accordingly.

Ultimately, it is important to keep in mind that there is no *guaranteed* way to increase your YouTube CPM, as the value of an ad is determined by a range of factors, including the quality and popularity of your content, the effectiveness of your monetization strategies, and the competitiveness of the advertising market. By implementing a range of strategies and continually improving your content and monetization strategies, you may be able to increase your YouTube CPM over time.

CHAPTER 4: ADS! ADS EVERYWHERE!

I'm sure you have seen the ads all across your YouTube videos (if you do not pay for premium or have an ad blocker extension). In this chapter we will look at the different types of ads in order to both better understand them and to help utilize them in your monetization path.

The different types of YouTube ads include are varied and seemingly they continue to use more and more intrusive types as the years go on. Even ad blockers are becoming worthless against the blight of advertisement. That being said, if you are a creator, your attitude towards ads may slowly change. Below I have set out the types of ads you may/will encounter throughout your journey.

I would recommend reading my descriptions throughout my series and any additional material you may uncover to understanding advertisement as much as you can. Understanding the ads can ultimately help you better plan your content to best suit both yours and your audience's needs. Below I will discuss the types of ads you can find on YouTube which may help you create content that can benifit from these specific types.

Skippable In-Stream Ads

Skippable in-stream ads are a type of YouTube ad that plays before, during, or after the main video and gives viewers the option to skip the ad after 5 seconds. These ads are an effective way for advertisers to reach their target audience and promote their products or services. When a viewer clicks on a video to watch, the skippable in-stream ad will play before the main video. The viewer has the option to skip the ad and proceed to the main video, or to watch the entire ad. If the viewer chooses to skip the ad, they will not be charged for the ad and the advertiser will not be charged for the ad impressions.

Skippable in-stream ads are a popular choice for advertisers because they allow the viewer to decide whether or not they want to watch the ad. This means that the viewer is more likely to watch the ad if they are interested in the product or service being advertised. Advertisers can also target their ads to specific demographics or interests, which can increase the likelihood that the ad will be watched.

As well as giving viewers the option to skip the ad, skippable in-stream ads also allow advertisers to track the number of ad impressions and the number of times the ad was skipped. This information can be useful for advertisers to understand how effective their ad campaign is and make adjustments as needed.

Non-Skippable In-Stream Ads

Aren't these just the *best? Non-skippable in-stream ads* are a type of YouTube ad that must be watched in their entirety before the main video can be accessed. These ads are an effective way for advertisers to reach their target audience and promote their products or services. When a viewer clicks on a video to watch, the non-skippable in-stream ad will play before the main video. The viewer does not have the option to skip the ad and must watch the entire ad before being able to access the main video.

Similiar to the skippable ads, non-skippable in-stream ads are a popular choice for advertisers because they ensure that the ad will be watched by the viewer. This can be particularly useful for advertisers who want to convey a specific message or call to action in their ad. Advertisers can also target their ads to specific demographics or interests, which can increase the likelihood that the ad will be watched.

Discovery ads

Discovery ads are an ad that appear next to related videos, search results, or on the YouTube homepage. You may have noticed these when being recommended videos. These ads are an effective way for advertisers to reach their target audience and promote their products or services.

Discovery ads can be either skippable or non-skippable. Skippable discovery ads allow the viewer to skip the ad after 5 seconds, while non-skippable discovery ads must be watched in their entirety before the main video can be accessed. Advertisers can choose the type of discovery ad that best fits their needs and goals.

These advertisement types are a very common choice for advertisers as they allow the viewer to discover new products or services that they may be interested in. These ads appear next to related videos, search results, or on the YouTube homepage, making them easy for viewers to find. Advertisers can also target their ads to specific demographics or interests, which can increase the likelihood that the ad will be watched.

Though it's primary function is showing the viewer new products or services, discovery ads also allow advertisers to track the number of ad impressions and the number of times the ad was watched or skipped. This information can be useful for advertisers to understand how effective their ad campaign is and make adjustments as needed which may be useful for you, depending on the deals you may get through advertises in the future.

Bumper Ads

Often *very* unpopular with viewers, *bumper ads* are a type of YouTube ad that are short, non-skippable ads that are usually 6 seconds or shorter. These ads are an effective way for advertisers to reach their target audience and promote their products or services.

Bumper ads are played before, during, or after the main video and must be watched in their entirety. They are designed to be quick and attention-grabbing, and are meant to leave a lasting impression on the viewer. Advertisers can use bumper ads to convey a specific message or call to action in a short amount of time.

Bumper ads are a somewhat unique option for advertisers because they allow the viewer to quickly absorb the message or call to action. These ads are also useful for advertisers who want to reach a wide audience, as they are played before, during, or after the main video. Advertisers can also target their ads to specific demographics or interests, which can increase the likelihood that the ad will be watched.

As a result of being quick and attention-grabbing, bumper ads also allow advertisers to track the number of ad impressions and the number of times the ad was watched. This information can be useful for advertisers to understand how effective their ad campaign is and make adjustments as needed.

Sponsored Cards

Sponsored cards are a type of YouTube ad that are interactive cards that appear during a video and provide more information about a product or service. These ads are an effective way for advertisers to reach their target audience and promote their products or services.

Sponsored cards appear as a small icon in the corner of the video player, and the viewer can click on the icon to view the card. The card contains more information about the product or service being advertised, such as a description, images, and a link to the advertiser's website. Sponsored cards are designed to be informative and interactive, and are meant to encourage the viewer to learn more about the product or service.

Overlay Ads

Overlay ads are a type of YouTube ad that are semi-transparent ads that appear on the bottom 20% of the video player. These ads are an effective way for advertisers to reach their target audience and promote their products or services.

These ads appear as a banner at the bottom of the video player, and the viewer can click on the banner to view the ad.

The ad contains more information about the product or service being advertised, such as a description, images, and a link to the advertiser's website. Overlay ads are designed to be unobtrusive and easy for the viewer to interact with.

They allow the viewer to easily access more information about the product or service without interrupting their viewing experience. These ads are also useful for advertisers who want to reach a specific audience, as they can target their ads to specific demographics or interests.

Further to being unobtrusive and easy to interact with, overlay ads also allow advertisers to track the number of ad impressions and the number of times the ad was viewed. This information can be useful for advertisers to understand how effective their ad campaign is and make adjustments as needed.

Display Ads

Display ads are a type of YouTube ad that are banner ads that appear on the YouTube website. These ads are an effective way for advertisers to reach their target audience and promote their products or services.

Display ads appear as banner ads on the YouTube website, and the viewer can click on the banner to view the ad. The ad contains more information about the product or service being advertised, such as a description, images, and a link to the advertiser's website. Display ads are designed to be eye-catching and easy for the viewer to interact with.

I would argue that display ads are a popular choice for current advertisers because they allow the viewer to easily access more information about the product or service without interrupting their browsing experience. These ads are also useful for advertisers who want to reach a specific audience, as they can target their ads to specific demographics or interests.

Video Bumpers

Video bumpers are short video ads that play before, after, or during a video break. These ads are an effective way for advertisers to reach their target audience and promote their products or services.

Video bumpers *must* be watched in their entirety. They are

designed to be quick and attention-grabbing, and are meant to leave a lasting impression on the viewer. Advertisers can use video bumpers to convey a specific message or call to action in a short amount of time. Advertisers can also target their ads to specific demographics or interests, which can increase the likelihood that the ad will be watched.

Like a number of the other forms of advertisement, video bumpers also allow advertisers to track the number of ad impressions and the number of times the ad was watched. This information can be useful for advertisers to understand how effective their ad campaign is and make adjustments as needed.

Outstream Ads

Finally, we have *outstream ads*. Outstream ads are ads that play on websites and apps other than YouTube, such as in a mobile app or on a website. These ads are an effective way for advertisers to reach their target audience and promote their products or services.

Outstream ads can be either skippable or non-skippable. Skippable outstream ads allow the viewer to skip the ad after 5 seconds, while non-skippable outstream ads must be watched in their entirety before the main video can be accessed. Advertisers can choose the type of outstream ad that best fits their needs and goals.

I would argue that they have become an important tool for advertisers as they allow the viewer to discover new products or services that they may be interested in while they are browsing websites or using apps other than YouTube. These ads are also useful for advertisers who want to reach a specific audience, as they can target their ads to specific demographics or interests. The outstream ads also allow advertisers to track the number of ad impressions and the number of times the ad was watched or skipped, and much like Video Bumpers, this information can be useful for advertisers to understand how effective their ad campaign is and make adjustments as needed.

CHAPTER 5: ALTERNATIVE WAYS OF MAKING MONEY

Okay, now we understand how YouTube advertises and potentially how we can customize videos to support these advertisements. As I mentioned earlier, Adsense can be fantastic, but in this book, I want to discuss alternative ways as well, focusing on our loyal audience and providing them something of value (and making us some money along the way).

Sponsorships

Sponsorship deals are a *popular/great* way to make money on

YouTube, and they can be a large source of income for creators who have a strong and engaged audience. In this chapter, we'll explore the ins and outs of sponsorship deals on YouTube and provide tips for finding and securing these lucrative partnerships.

First, let's start with the basics. A sponsorship deal is a partnership between a creator and a brand in which the brand pays the creator to promote their products or services in their videos. These deals can take various forms, such as sponsored video content, product placements, or sponsored social media posts.

To find sponsorship opportunities, you can reach out to brands directly or join an influencer marketing platform that connects creators with brands looking for partnerships. When reaching out to brands or applying for sponsorship opportunities, it's important to have a clear and professional pitch that highlights your audience demographics and engagement, as well as your past successes and relevant experience.

If you are interested in pursuing a sponsorship deal with a particular brand, there are a few things you can do to increase your chances of success.

Research the brand

Learn as much as you can about the brand and its target market to determine whether your content aligns with the brand's values and goals.

Create a professional pitch

Prepare a professional pitch that outlines the value you can offer to the brand, including your audience demographics, engagement levels, and any relevant past collaborations or achievements.

Consider offering a trial period

Some brands may be hesitant to commit to a long-term sponsorship without seeing the results first. Consider offering a trial period to give the brand a taste of what you can offer.

Keep an eye out for sponsored content opportunities

Some brands may offer sponsored content opportunities through their own channels or through third-party platforms. Keep an eye out for these opportunities and consider applying if you think your content aligns with the brand's goals.

As always, I love giving practical examples. Below I have included a potential email template you could use to send to a brand you may be interested in having sponsor you. The below email is specifically for a "Let's Play" channel interested in a PC company, like our earlier example. Note, this can also be used in our following chapter regarding more long-term Brand Partnerships.

Dear [Brand],

I am writing to express my interest in exploring a brand sponsorship opportunity with your company.

I am the creator of the [YouTube channel name] channel, which is focused on [channel content]. My channel currently has [number] subscribers and [number] views, and my audience is primarily made up of [target audience demographics].

I believe that my channel aligns well with your brand's values and goals, and I am confident that a sponsorship partnership would be beneficial for both of us. In addition to the exposure and brand awareness that my channel can offer, I am also able to offer [specific value or benefit that you can offer to the brand].

I would be happy to discuss the details of a potential sponsorship partnership with you further. Please let me know if you are interested in exploring this opportunity, and I will provide more information about my channel and my audience.

Thank you for considering my proposal.

Sincerely, [Your name]

Once you secure a sponsorship deal, it's important to *follow through* on your end of the agreement and deliver high-quality content that promotes the brand's products or services in an authentic and transparent way. It's also important to be transparent with your audience about sponsored content and disclose any sponsored partnerships in accordance with YouTube's guidelines and any applicable laws.

Brand Partnerships

Similar to sponsorship deals, *brand partnerships* are a type of sponsorship on YouTube that are long-term collaborations between a brand and a creator, where the creator promotes the brand's products or services in exchange for compensation. These partnerships can take many forms, such as sponsored videos, social media posts, or product placements. Brand partnerships are an effective way for brands to reach their target audience and promote their products or services, and they can also be a lucrative source of income for creators.

Brand partnerships are a popular choice for both brands and creators because they allow for a more in-depth collaboration between the two parties. This can lead to more authentic and engaging content for the viewer, and it can also help build trust between the viewer and the brand. Brand partnerships are also useful for brands because they allow the brand to reach a specific audience, as they can target their ads to specific demographics or interests.

They are a great way to promote a product or service, brand partnerships, allowing brands to track the number of ad impressions and the number of times the content was viewed or engaged with. This information can be useful for brands to understand how effective their ad campaign is and make adjustments as needed.

For creators, brand partnerships can be a lucrative way to make money on YouTube. Creators can negotiate a fair fee for their time and effort, and they can also earn additional income through ad revenue if the content is monetized. Brand partnerships can also help creators expand their audience and reach new viewers.

Ultimately, I have found that brand partnerships are a useful tool for both brands and creators to reach their target audience and promote products or services on YouTube. They offer a way for brands to showcase their products or services in a more in-depth and authentic way, and they can also be a lucrative source of income for creators.

Product Placement

Something you may have noticed when not done well, *Product placements* are a type of sponsorship on YouTube where a brand's product or service is featured in a YouTube video in a natural way. This can involve the creator using the product in their video or simply mentioning the product. Product placements are an effective way for brands to reach their target audience and promote their products or services.

Product placements are a popular choice for brands because they allow the viewer to see the product being used in a natural way. This can help build trust with the viewer and increase the likelihood that they will be interested in purchasing the product. Product placements are also useful for brands because they allow the brand to reach a specific audience, as they can target their placements to specific demographics or interests.

As well as being a natural way to promote a product or service, product placements also allow brands to track the number of ad impressions and the number of times the product was mentioned or shown. This information can be useful for brands to understand how effective their ad campaign is and make adjustments as needed.

Generally speaking, product placements are a useful tool for brands to reach their target audience and promote their products or services on YouTube. They offer a way for brands to reach viewers who are interested in seeing products being used in a natural way, and they also allow brands to track the effectiveness of their ad campaigns.

Though product placements can be a good way to monetize your YouTube videos, but it is important to make sure that they feel *natural* and do not disrupt the viewing experience for your audience. Here are some tips to help you make product placements feel natural in your videos:

Choose products that align with your content and audience

Choose products that are relevant to your content and that your audience is likely to be interested in. This will help make the product placement feel more natural and less intrusive.

Integrate the product into your content

Rather than simply showing the product and talking about it, try to integrate it into your content in a natural way. For example, if you are reviewing a product, you could use it as part of your demonstration or show how it fits into your daily routine.

Be transparent

It is important to be transparent with your audience about your relationship with the brand. Disclose any sponsored content or product placements in your video description or in the video itself.

Avoid overdoing it

While product placements can be a good source of income, it is important to avoid overdoing it. Too many product placements can be overwhelming for your audience and may turn them off.

CHAPTER 6: BUT WAIT, THERE'S MORE!

Let's continue with our alternative ways to make money.

Sponsored Live Streams

Sponsored live streams are a type of sponsorship on YouTube where a brand pays a creator to do a live stream promoting their product or service. These live streams are an effective way for brands to reach their target audience and promote their products or services, and they can also be a lucrative source of income for creators.

Sponsored live streams have become a popular choice for brands in 2023 because they allow the creator to showcase the product or service in a more interactive and engaging way. This can help build trust with the viewer and increase the likelihood that they will be interested in purchasing the product. Sponsored live streams are also useful for brands because they allow the brand to reach a specific audience, as they can target their ads to specific demographics or interests.

For us creators, sponsored live streams can be a lucrative way to make money on YouTube. Creators can negotiate a fair fee for their time and effort, and they can also earn additional income through ad revenue if the live stream is monetized. Sponsored live streams can also help creators expand their audience and reach new viewers.

I have also mentioned in my other titles, a great way to make additional content is to clip pieces of these live streams and upload them as separate videos.

Sponsored Social Media Posts

Something that I have slowly noticed is falling 'Out of fashion' but definitely still lucrative to the right creators are *sponsored social media posts.* Sponsored social media posts are a type of sponsorship on YouTube where a brand pays a creator to promote their product or service on social media platforms such as Instagram or Twitter. These sponsored posts are an effective way for brands to reach their target audience and promote their products or services, and they can also be a lucrative source of income for creators.

Sponsored social media posts are a popular choice for brands because they allow the creator to showcase the product or service in a more personal and (seemingly) authentic way. This can help build trust with the viewer and increase the likelihood that they will be interested in purchasing the product. Sponsored social media posts are also useful for brands because they allow the brand to reach a specific audience, as they can target their ads to specific demographics or interests.

From an analytical perspective, sponsored social media posts allow brands to track the number of ad impressions and the amount of engagement the post receives. This information can be useful for brands to understand how effective their ad campaign is and make adjustments as needed.

For YouTubers, sponsored social media posts can be a lucrative way to make money on their channels, but as I mentioned, you will need to have it match your own branding specifically. When done right, YouTubers can negotiate a *great fee* for their time and effort, and they can also earn additional income through ad revenue if the post is monetized. Sponsored social media posts can also help creators expand their audience and reach new viewers.

Patreon

Patreon is a difficult revenue stream to capture. You need to provide a lot of value to your audience and in my opinion your fanbase has to be both *very large* and *very loyal*. That being said, when done right, it can essentially give you a living wage so you can focus on your channel

Well what is it? Patreon is a popular platform that allows creators to earn money from their fans on a recurring basis. In this chapter, we'll explore the ins and outs of Patreon on YouTube and provide tips for maximizing your earnings through this platform.

Patreon is a subscription-based platform that allows creators to offer exclusive content and perks to their supporters, who contribute small amounts of money on a regular basis. Creators can offer a variety of rewards and tiers to their supporters, such as access to exclusive videos, behind-the-scenes content, or personalized shoutouts.

To start earning money through Patreon, you must first set up a Patreon account and create a campaign outlining the rewards and tiers you will offer to your supporters. It's important to clearly communicate the value of your rewards and the benefits of supporting you on Patreon.

Once your campaign is set up, you can promote it to your audience through your YouTube videos and social media channels. It's also a good idea to regularly engage with your supporters and thank them for their support, as this can help encourage them to continue supporting you on Patreon.

As I mentioned, you will need a large/loyal audience, but even then you will need to showcase the following to recieve any real amount of money.

Offer exclusive content to your Patreon supporters

One way to encourage people to become Patreon supporters is by offering exclusive content that is only available to supporters. This could include behind-the-scenes videos, early access to new content, or Q&A sessions.

Communicate the value of supporting you on Patreon

Make sure to clearly communicate the value of supporting you on Patreon to your viewers. Explain how their support will help you create more content and what they can expect in return for their support.

Set clear tiers and rewards for supporters

Offer different tiers of support with corresponding rewards to encourage people to support you at higher levels. These rewards could include access to exclusive content, personalized shoutouts, or personalized merchandise.

Engage with your Patreon supporters

Make sure to regularly engage with your Patreon supporters, whether through comments, social media, or live streams. This will help build a sense of community and encourage them to continue supporting you.

Promote your Patreon page regularly

Regularly promote your Patreon page to your YouTube audience, both through your videos and through social media. This will help increase awareness and encourage more people to become supporters.

Make it easy for viewers to support you

Make sure that your Patreon page is easy to find and navigate, and include links to it in your video descriptions and on your social media profiles.

Experiment with different rewards and tiers

Don't be afraid to experiment with different rewards and tiers to find out what works best for your audience. This could involve adding new rewards or changing the levels of support.

Affiliate Marketing

Affiliate marketing is a monetization method that allows creators to earn a commission by promoting products or services on their YouTube channel. In this chapter, we'll explore the ins and outs of affiliate marketing on YouTube and provide tips for maximizing your earnings through this monetization method. It is similar to product placement but through an affiliate marketing website instead of the brand directly.

Basically, affiliate marketing involves promoting products or services on your YouTube channel and earning a commission for every sale made through a unique affiliate link. To participate in affiliate marketing, you must first join an affiliate program, such as Amazon Associates or Commission Junction, and apply to promote specific products or services.

To maximize your earnings through affiliate marketing, it's important to choose products or services that align with your brand and audience and to promote them in a genuine and transparent way. It's also a good idea to regularly review and update the products or services you are promoting to ensure that they are still relevant and useful to your audience.

Remember that YouTube is not the only place to promote your products. Promoting products or services on your YouTube videos, you can also promote them through your social media channels and website. By following these tips and best practices, you can effectively use affiliate marketing to supplement your income on YouTube and provide valuable recommendations to your audience.

CHAPTER 7: SELL! SELL! SELL!

Merchandise

Another one of my favorites is *merchandising.* Merchandising is another way creators can make money on YouTube, and it can be particularly lucrative for those with a strong and loyal audience. In this chapter, we'll delve into the details of merchandising on YouTube and provide tips for maximizing your earnings through this monetization method.

First, let's look at the *essentials.*

Merchandising on YouTube involves creating and selling physical products, such as t-shirts, hats, or stickers, through your YouTube channel. To sell merchandise, you'll need to set up a merchandise shelf in your channel's "About" section and link to an online store or platform where your merchandise can be purchased. You can either create the products yourself or work with a manufacturer or retailer to produce and distribute the merchandise on your behalf. It's important to choose high-quality products that align with your brand and appeal to your target audience.

Once you have your merchandise set up, you can promote it to your audience through your YouTube videos and social media channels. Offering special deals or discounts to your most loyal supporters can also encourage them to purchase your merchandise. Generally I find it best to just do this at either the beginning or end of your videos.

There are many different *types* of merchandise that you can sell on YouTube to monetize your channel. Some popular options include:

T-shirts

T-shirts are a classic and versatile option that can be customized with your channel's branding or designs. This is the go to for merchandise and for a reason. T-Shirts are fantastic as not only are they low cost, they provide branding for your business/brand/channel and pushes you into the zeitgeist.

Stickers

Stickers are a fun and affordable option that can be used to promote your channel or as a giveaway for your audience. Though they are quite cheap, I have found these to be great way to earn additional income.

Also see:

Mugs

Phone cases

Hats

Posters

Merchandising Options

Shopify

There are a lot of merchandising options so it is important to find one that works with your niche and offers the best fit. One that I know a lot of people have had success with in 2023 is Shopify. Shopify is an e-commerce platform that allows businesses to create and manage an online store. As a YouTube creator, you can monetize your channel by partnering with Shopify and joining their partnership program.

Here's how it works:

Sign up for the Shopify Affiliate Program

To join the Shopify partnership program, you will need to sign up for the Shopify Affiliate Program. This will give you access to a range of resources and tools to help you promote Shopify to your audience and earn commissions on any sales that you generate.

Promote Shopify to your audience

Once you have signed up for the Shopify Affiliate Program, you can start promoting Shopify to your audience through your YouTube videos. You can do this by mentioning Shopify in your videos, sharing your own experiences with the platform, and sharing links to the Shopify website.

Earn commissions on sales

When someone clicks on one of your affiliate links and makes a purchase on the Shopify website, you will earn a commission on the sale. The commission rate will depend on the products that are purchased, but you can typically expect to earn a percentage of the sale price.

Track your earnings

You can track your earnings and see how well your affiliate links are performing through the Shopify Affiliate Program dashboard. This will help you see what is working and what you can improve upon.

As you can see, by partnering with Shopify and joining their partnership program, you can monetize your YouTube channel by promoting the platform to your audience and earning commissions on any sales that you generate. By offering value to your audience and promoting high-quality products, you can build trust and credibility with your audience, which can help you earn more from your affiliate links.

Creating Influence Content

The term "Influencer" has received a bad rap over the last couple of years (and probably for good reason) but I do believe there is still money to be made, without forfeiting your dignity and reputation.

Creating *influencer content* for brands is a monetization method that involves getting hired by companies and brands as an influencer to create original content for them. As an influencer, you will be responsible for promoting the brand's products or services to your audience through sponsored content on your YouTube channel.

To be successful as an influencer on YouTube, it is important to have a loyal following and a clear niche or community that you are serving with your videos. Companies and brands are more likely to hire influencers who have a dedicated and engaged audience, as this can help them reach a wider audience and increase their sales.

To start creating influencer content for brands, you can reach out to companies and brands that align with your values and content and pitch them on the idea of working together. You can also work with influencer marketing agencies to help you find brand partnerships.

Just remember, when creating influencer content for brands, it's important to be transparent and disclose any sponsored content to your audience. This will help you maintain the trust and credibility of your audience and ensure that you are following YouTube's guidelines for sponsored content.

Promotion of Your Own Products

Promoting your *own products* or services is a monetization method that involves using your videos to educate viewers about the products or services that you offer. This can be a powerful way to make money on YouTube, as it allows you to use your platform to drive sales and generate revenue for your business.

To start promoting your products or services on YouTube, you will need to create educational and informative videos that showcase the benefits of your products or services. These videos can be used to demonstrate how your products or services can solve the problems or meet the needs of your target audience.

It's important to be mindful of YouTube's guidelines for promotional content and to disclose any sponsored or promotional videos to your audience. This will help you maintain the trust and credibility of your audience and ensure that you are following YouTube's policies.

Many YouTube influencers have found success with this monetization method, as it allows them to use their platform to build their brand and reach a wider audience. By promoting your own products or services on YouTube, you can increase your income and achieve financial success on the platform.

Generally speaking, promoting your own products or services on YouTube is a monetization method that involves using your videos to educate viewers about the products or services that you offer. By creating informative and engaging videos and following YouTube's guidelines for promotional content, you can increase your income and achieve financial success on the platform.

Creating an Online Course

I'm sure you have seen the many, *many* 'influencers' across the social media platforms trying to sell you their online courses to earn $1,000/day and other unbelievable claims. However, if done both correctly and *ethically*, creating an online course can be a great way to monetize your expertise and share it with a wider audience on YouTube.

By offering a course on a topic that you are passionate about and have expertise in, you can generate income and build a successful business on the platform.

Here is a very basic step-by-step guide on how to create an online course on YouTube. Remember, we are looking to provide value to our audience so really do try to provide a polished piece of content that will better their lives.

Identify a topic for your course

The first step in creating an online course is to choose a topic that you are passionate about and have expertise in. It should be something that is in demand and that you can provide valuable insights and information on. Consider your interests, skills, and knowledge, and think about how you can use them to create a course that will be valuable to learners.

Create a course outline

Once you have chosen a topic for your course, it is important to organize your material into a clear and logical structure. Break the course into smaller chunks or modules, and include activities and assessments to help learners engage with the material and retain the information. This will make it easier for learners to follow and understand the material, and it will help you to deliver the course effectively.

Record and edit your course

The next step is to record and edit your course. Use a high-quality microphone and camera to capture your voice and image, and consider using video editing software to enhance the visual elements of your course, such as slides, images, and animations. By investing in good equipment and editing software, you can create a professional and engaging course that will appeal to learners.

Promote your course

Once your course is complete, it is important to promote it to reach a wider audience. Use your YouTube channel and social media to share information about your course, and consider offering a discount or free preview to attract potential learners. By promoting your course effectively, you can build a significant following and generate income from your course.

Deliver your course

The final step is to make your course available for purchase on YouTube. You can use a platform such as Teachable or Udemy to host your course and manage payment and enrollment. By delivering your course through a reputable platform, you can ensure that your course is accessible and easy for learners to purchase and access.

Again, it is important to keep in mind that creating an online course requires time, effort, and dedication, and it may take some time to build up a significant following and generate significant income. Many people rush into this option and it gives their channel a bad reputation as online courses are often associated with pyramid schemes and charlatans. However, by continuously improving and promoting your course, you can build a successful business and make money on YouTube.

CHAPTER 8: YOUTUBE EXTRAS

Super Chat and Super Stickers

These features below are used by successful YouTubers to generate quite a lot of additional income.

Super Chat and *Super Stickers* are features on YouTube that allow viewers to engage and interact with creators more prominently during live streams. Super Chat allows viewers to purchase a chat message that is highlighted within the chat, while Super Stickers allow viewers to purchase a static or animated image that appears in the live chat feed.

These features can be a valuable source of income for creators, as they give viewers the opportunity to show their support and appreciation for the content being produced. Live streams can be surprisingly profitable if creators put in the time and effort to engage with their audience and make the most of these monetization opportunities.

Nick Nimmin, a YouTube educator with over 500K subscribers, is a great example of a creator who has successfully used Super Chat and Super Stickers to monetize his live streams. His channel is an excellent resource for anyone looking for tips and tricks on how to make the most of live streams on YouTube.

Ultimately, this may be something to look at in the future if you are just starting out but keep them in mind! Super Chat and Super Stickers are valuable monetization tools for creators on YouTube, as they allow viewers to show their support and engage with the content being produced. By utilizing these features and engaging with their audience during live streams, creators can increase their income and achieve financial success on the platform.

Once you are ready, below I have included a few practical tips for making money with Superchat on YouTube.

Use Superchat during live streams

Superchat is a feature that allows viewers to donate money to a creator during a live stream. To make money with Superchat, make sure to use it during your live streams. You can announce that you are using Superchat and encourage your viewers to donate.

Set up tiered Superchat messages

You can set up tiered Superchat messages, where viewers can choose to donate different amounts of money and receive different perks or rewards in return. This can encourage viewers to donate more money and help you make more money with Superchat.

Engage with your Superchat donors

Make sure to thank your Superchat donors and engage with them during your live streams. This can help build a sense of community and encourage more people to donate.

Promote your Superchat

Make sure to promote your Superchat feature to your audience, both during your live streams and on social media. This will help increase awareness and encourage more people to donate.

Consider offering exclusive content to Superchat donors

You can also consider offering exclusive content to your Superchat donors as a way to encourage them to donate. This could be access to a special live stream, a Q&A session, or early access to new content.

Monitor your Superchat revenue

Keep track of your Superchat revenue and use it as a way to gauge the success of your live streams. This can help you understand what works and what doesn't and make adjustments as needed.

YouTube Premium

The second option is utilizing *YouTube Premium*. YouTube Premium is a subscription service that allows users to watch videos without ads and access other premium content on the platform. As a creator, you can make money through YouTube Premium by offering content that is available exclusively to YouTube Premium subscribers. In this chapter, we'll explore the ins and outs of YouTube Premium and provide tips for maximizing your earnings through this monetization method.

YouTube Premium is a subscription service that allows users to watch videos without ads and access other premium content, such as original series and movies, on the platform. As a creator, you can offer content that is available exclusively to YouTube Premium subscribers, such as behind-the-scenes footage or early access to your videos.

To make money through YouTube Premium, you must first enable monetization for your channel and meet the eligibility requirements for the YouTube Partner Program. Once you have met these requirements, you can apply to participate in the YouTube Premium Partner Program by going to the "Monetization" tab in the "Channel" section of YouTube Studio.

To maximize your earnings through YouTube Premium, it's important to create high-quality content that is exclusive to YouTube Premium subscribers and promote your premium content to your audience. It's also a good idea to regularly engage with your premium subscribers and thank them for their support.

YouTube Channel Memberships

At first, this was seen almost as a *dirty* thing to ask for in the YouTube community, however with the rise in popularity of platforms such as *Twitch, YouTube channel memberships* have become a great monetization method. It allows creators to offer exclusive content and perks to their subscribers who pay a monthly fee to join their channel. In this chapter, we'll explore the ins and outs of YouTube channel memberships and provide tips for maximizing your earnings through this monetization method.

First, let's start with the basics. YouTube channel memberships are a subscription-based service that allows creators to offer exclusive content and perks to their subscribers who pay a monthly fee to join their channel. These perks can include access to exclusive videos, behind-the-scenes content, or personalized shoutouts.

To offer channel memberships, you must first enable monetization for your channel and meet the eligibility requirements for the YouTube Partner Program. Once you have met these requirements, you can apply to participate in the YouTube Channel Memberships program by going to the "Monetization" tab in the "Channel" section of YouTube Studio.

To maximize your earnings through YouTube channel memberships, it's important to create high-quality and exclusive content that is worth the monthly fee for your subscribers. It's also a good idea to regularly engage with your channel members and thank them for their support.

CHAPTER 9: DON'T FORGET

Tax in USA

Just a side note, if (when!) you are successful and you are making money on YouTube in the United States, you will need to report your earnings to the Internal Revenue Service (IRS) and pay taxes on your income. Here are a few tax-related considerations to keep in mind that I had to look into when I first started making money.

Determine your tax filing status

Your tax filing status determines your tax bracket and the amount of taxes you owe. It's important to accurately determine your tax filing status, which can be single, married filing jointly, married filing separately, or head of household.

Keep track of your earnings

It's important to keep accurate records of your earnings from YouTube, as you will need to report them on your tax return. This includes keeping track of any expenses you incur related to your YouTube channel, as these may be deductible on your tax return.

Determine your tax liability

Your tax liability is the amount of taxes you owe based on your income and filing status. You may be required to make estimated tax payments if you expect to owe more than $1,000 in taxes for the year.

Consider hiring a tax professional

If you are unsure about how to handle the tax implications of your YouTube earnings, it may be a good idea to hire a tax professional to help you navigate the process. A tax professional can provide guidance on how to report your earnings and claim any deductions or credits you may be eligible for.

CONCLUSION

As always, I hope I have provided a semi-comprehensive overview of the various ways in which you can monetize your YouTube channel. From advertising and sponsorships to merchandise and fan funding, there are many options available to creators looking to turn their passion into a profitable business.

Remember, the one thing I try to preach is that by focusing on building a strong and engaged audience, creating high-quality and relevant content, and leveraging the right monetization strategies, you can turn your YouTube channel into a successful and profitable venture. You should always be proactive, be willing to try new things, and above all, have patience. It takes time and effort to build a successful YouTube channel, but with the right approach, you can turn your passion into a profitable business.

THANK YOU READERS

Again, thank you very much for reading this far and for your continued support. As an author I am hoping to evolve as you do as a content creator.

I will continue to release titles in this series, eventually writing very specific titles for individual niches, creating in-depth manuals to help you succeed.

But until then, all my love.

Ben.

P.s if you enjoyed my title, please do not forget to give me a great rating on Amazon!

www.ingramcontent.com/pod-product-compliance
Lightning Source LLC
Chambersburg PA
CBHW070301220526
45465CB00004B/1700